The Blessings

of the

Beatitudes

By Pastor John Pennell

Calvary Chapel of Lake Villa

Calvary Chapel of Lake Villa

38451 N. Fairfield Rd.

Lake Villa, IL 60046

847-265-0646 / www.cclv.org

The Blessings of the Beatitudes

by Pastor John Pennell

2013 The Cleansing Word Publishers

P.O. Box 646, Lake Villa, IL 60046

847-265-0646

www.cclv.org

Unless otherwise indicated, all Scripture quotations are taken from the New King James Version of the Bible. Translations, emendations, amplifications and para-phrases are by the author.

Front Cover: photo by Bud Carlson, from the area where Jesus might have preached the Sermon of the Mount.

Back Cover: photo by "Welsh Studios of Fox Lake"

Printed in the United States of America

Preface

"The Sermon on the Mount covers Matthew chapters 5-7, and was preached by Jesus from a mount overlooking the Sea of Galilee. It contains 107 verses and is a miracle of concision and wisdom. Jesus introduces this sermon with the 'Beatitudes' which essentially gives to us the "blueprint" for the Christian life.

They begin with the inability of man to do anything that will earn him salvation – from the hunger and thirst that accompany those who realize they need Jesus' righteousness for salvation – to the inevitable persecution from the world and the ultimate glory in heaven for all possessors of salvation as God's children.

Pastor John has captured this essential progression in this booklet which, once read, will open to the understanding God's plan of salvation and the glorious destination He has for all who embrace the gospel of His Son Jesus Christ."

Pastor Phil Ballmaier

Calvary Chapel of Elk Grove, IL

Contents

Acknowledgements

I realize that I am a compilation of a lot of different people who have influenced my life. Some of these people I have known very dearly, while others have impacted me through their writings and teachings.

I am very thankful for the Lord's work in my parent's lives, for without their example of faith, I know that I would not be the man that I am today. To have a dad who came to faith in his late twenties and in less than ten years was preaching the gospel of Jesus Christ - let's just say that his boldness still teaches me to this day.

I became a Calvary Chapel pastor largely because of the influences of Pastor Chuck Smith, Pastor Carl Westerlund, Pastor L. E. Romaine, Pastor Ray Snook and Dr. David Hocking. These men not only taught me in the classroom, but also exemplified what it means to live out your faith.

There is none more dear to me than my family. To my beautiful wife, Lily, your sweet love for Jesus and our family continues to be a great anchor for our family. If it were not for your encouragement, I would have never gone to the School of Ministry at Calvary Chapel of Costa Mesa. To our daughter, Melissa, thank you for all your hard editing work. You help me sound smarter than I actually am. To our son, John, watching Jesus' work in your life has strengthened my own faith, knowing that God does *exceedingly abundantly above all that we ask or think (Eph 3:20).*

Also to my dear friends, Jon Marquardt and Dave Dew, your additional editing skills have been greatly appreciated.

Finally, to Calvary Chapel of Lake Villa, thank you for allowing me to be your pastor for these past fourteen years.

Introduction

In chapter five of Matthew's gospel, we have what is known to us as The Beatitudes, which consists of eight declarations of blessedness made by Jesus at the beginning of the Sermon on the Mount.

Each of the eight beatitudes begins with the words, *"Blessed are."* The Greek word translated as *blessed* is *makarios* (mak-ar`-ee-os). It speaks about having a **spiritual well-being and prosperity, a deep joy of the soul.* Each Beatitude reveals a believer's present position and his future reward.

From a worldly perspective, the *blessed* are those who are fortunate, well-off or happy. However, from the Biblical perspective, they are those who have found this *spiritual well-being and prosperity; this deep joy of the soul.*

When considering The Beatitudes, we may ask, "How can a man or a woman be considered *blessed* if they are *poor, mourning, meek, hungry* or *thirsty; persecuted* or *reviled?* Perhaps the answer to this question is found in the very first beatitude concerning the poor in spirit.

Matthew 5:1 And seeing the multitudes, He went up on a mountain, and when He was seated His disciples came to Him. 2 Then He opened His mouth and taught them, saying:

* From Nelson's Illustrated Bible Dictionary, © 1986, Thomas Nelson Publishers

Blessed are the Poor in Spirit

Matthew 5:3 Blessed are the poor in spirit, for theirs is the kingdom of God.

This first declaration of blessedness made by Jesus is given to those of us who are the *poor in spirit.*

There were two Greek words that could have been used to describe the *poor in spirit.*

The first word is *penes* (pen`-ace). It speaks about a laborer, someone who has to work for his daily bread. They are those who have no extra cash at the end of the week, but when the week has ended, their work and toil has supplied all their needs.

The second word is *ptochos* (pto-khos`). It refers to someone who is poor or destitute, such as a beggar. They are people who cannot make it without help from someone else. No matter how hard they try, they are simply incapable of supplying their daily needs.

This second Greek word is the word that Matthew used to describe the *poor in spirit.*

The word *spirit* speaks of our inner being or the immortal part of mankind. Being *poor in spirit* describes the condition of every man and woman on this earth. We are *the poor in spirit* because we cannot make it without help from Jesus.

Isa 59:1 Behold, the LORD's hand is not shortened, that it cannot save; nor His ear heavy, that it cannot hear. 2 But your iniquities (or sins) *have separated you from your God; and your sins have hidden His face from you, so that He will not hear.*

8

Our Father, knowing the condition of our spirits and the condition of our hearts, sent His only begotten Son to be the help that we all so desperately need.

The *poor in spirit* becomes *blessed* when a person recognizes his spiritual inability and comes humbly before Jesus confessing their sins. In doing so they find the forgiveness that can only come through Jesus Christ our Lord.

The *poor in spirit* is blessed with this *spiritual well-being and prosperity, a deep joy of the soul* because of Jesus' ability to save those who are unable to save themselves. It is through the salvation that Jesus has made available to us, that we can have this foretaste of blessedness, which will continue on into *the kingdom of heaven.* However, this blessing can only come through the recognition and confession of our sins, to the One who gave His life upon the cross.

Rom 10:9 that if you confess with your mouth the Lord Jesus and believe in your heart that God has raised Him from the dead, you will be saved. 10 For with the heart one believes unto righteousness, and with the mouth confession is made unto salvation. 11 For the Scripture says, "Whoever believes on Him will not be put to shame." 12 For there is no distinction between Jew and Greek, for the same Lord over all is rich to all who call upon Him. 13 For "whoever calls on the name of the LORD shall be saved."

Have you recognized that you are the *poor in spirit*? If so, the next step is to cry out in faith to Jesus. The kingdom of heaven then awaits you!

Blessed Are Those Who Mourn

Matthew 5:4 Blessed are those who mourn, for they shall be comforted.

This second of eight declarations of blessedness made by Jesus concerns those who *mourn*.

Mourning is something that we have all done on many different occasions in our lives. We can mourn over the loss of a job, the end of an era in life, changes in friends or circumstances and yes, of course, the death of a loved one.

We have all mourned in many different ways and circumstances, and we will mourn again in many other ways and circumstances. However, it is through Jesus that we can *mourn* with the hope of finding true *comfort*.

The Greek word that is translated as *comfort* is the compound word, *parakaleo* (para-k-al-eh`-o). *Para* means *near* or *alongside* and *kaleo* means *to call*. When we combine these two words it gives us a word that means *to call near*. So we have this picture of a comforter as someone calling us over and putting an arm of reassurance around us. In the context of our passage, we know that the One who draws near to us, to comfort us, is the Lord.

James 4:8a Draw near to God and He will draw near to you.

We have many examples in Scripture of the Tri-unity of the Godhead bringing comfort to our hearts. Such comfort establishes and multiplies the body of Christ. It gives us hope and causes us to become like-minded, and it also helps us in comforting others.

Our Savior Jesus comforts and establishes us.

2 Thess 2:16 Now may our Lord Jesus Christ Himself, and our God and Father, who has loved us and given us everlasting consolation and good hope by grace, 17 comfort your hearts and establish you in every good word and work.

The comfort of Holy Spirit helps to multiply the church.

Acts 9:31 Then the churches throughout all Judea, Galilee, and Samaria had peace and were edified. And walking in the fear of the Lord and in the comfort of the Holy Spirit, they were multiplied.

The Word of God and God Himself becomes our *comfort*.

Rom 15:4 For whatever things were written before were written for our learning, that we through the patience and comfort of the Scriptures might have hope. 5 Now may the God of patience and comfort grant you to be like-minded toward one another, according to Christ Jesus.

God's Word comforts us because it teaches us to have hope. Paul calls God *the God of patience and comfort*, and tells us that we should be like Him, by bringing *comfort* to others.

As part of the body of Christ, we will each have seasons when we will mourn. May we not only find our hope and comfort in seasons of mourning through Jesus Christ, but also help bring His comfort to those who mourn.

2 Cor 1:3 Blessed be the God and Father of our Lord Jesus Christ, the Father of mercies and God of all comfort, 4 who comforts us in all our tribulation, that we may be able to comfort those who are in any trouble, with the comfort with which we ourselves are comforted by God.

Blessed Are The Meek

Matthew 5:5 Blessed are the meek, for they shall inherit the earth.

In this third declaration of blessedness, there is the promise to those who are *meek*.

Perhaps we can envision how meekness could lead to the spiritual well-being of one's soul, but how does meekness lead to prosperity?

According to Webster's Dictionary, to be *meek* means to be *submissive* or *humble*. The Greek scholar Spiros Zodhiates adds *lowly* to this definition. Other words that could describe what it means to be meek are *gentleness, considerate*, or *unassuming*. Therefore, one who is *meek* could be described as one who is *submissive, humble, lowly, gentle, considerate and unassuming*.

These qualities don't seem to be the qualities of those who will inherit the earth. We might be more apt to think that *the aggressive* and *the self-assertive* will inherit the earth, but not *the meek*.

As I thought about examples from the Bible of those who were meek, two people immediately came to mind:

1. Moses

Num 12:3 Now the man Moses was very humble (KJV = very meek), more than all men who were on the face of the earth.

As the LORD dealt with Miriam and Aaron's rebellion, He said to them that His servant Moses is *"faithful in all My house. I speak with him face to face, even plainly, and not in dark sayings; and he sees the form of the LORD. Why then were you not afraid to speak against My servant Moses?"*

The fear of the LORD came upon Miriam and Aaron after she became leprous, but Moses revealed his *meekness* by praying for those who had cursed him. As a result God forgave them and healed Miriam.

2. Jesus

Matt 21:5 "Tell the daughter of Zion, 'Behold, your King is coming to you, lowly (KJV = *meek), and sitting on a donkey, a colt, the foal of a donkey.'"*

Jesus came *lowly, in gentleness, humbleness* and *meekness.* He who *being in the form of God, did not consider it robbery to be equal with God, but made Himself of no reputation, taking the form of a bondservant, and coming in the likeness of men. And being found in appearance as a man, He humbled Himself and became obedient to the point of death, even the death of the cross (Phil 2:6-9).*

In the light of God's Word, meekness is a poverty of spirit, the absence of boastfulness or pride; it is seeing ourselves in the light of Jesus, which brings a true revelation of ourselves. When we finally see God for who He is, we will then have a proper perspective of who we are.

This is so far from the world's philosophy. To the world *the meek* are looked down upon and sort of run over. The world will say to *the meek,* "You will never get anywhere, unless you are aggressive and self-assertive." But Jesus said, *"Blessed are the meek, for they shall inherit the earth."*

Can we be meek and humble like Moses or Jesus? Not in our own strength, but our Lord Jesus has said to us, *"Take My yoke upon you and learn from Me, for I am gentle and lowly in heart, and you will find rest for your souls" (Matt 11:29).*

Blessed Are the Hungry and Thirsty

Matthew 5:6 Blessed are those who hunger and thirst for righteousness, for they shall be filled.

In this fourth declaration of blessedness, Jesus promises that *those who hunger and thirst for righteousness shall be filled.*

In the book of Amos there is an interesting prophecy that foretold of a coming famine.

Amos 8:11 "Behold, the days are coming," says the Lord GOD, "That I will send a famine on the land, not a famine of bread, nor a thirst for water, but of hearing the words of the LORD."

This Old Testament prophecy seems to have been fulfilled during the four hundred years of silence between the Old and New Testaments. God stopped speaking to His people during this time and there developed a hunger and thirst in some of the people of Israel for the *hearing* of the *words of the LORD.*

As we consider the day in which we live, there once again seems to be a famine on the land *of hearing the words of the LORD.* We have many churches, but within the churches there are only a few believers who truly desire to hear *the words of the LORD.*

Those who *hunger and thirst for righteousness* are a minority rather than a majority within our churches today. The majority seems to be seeking their own pleasure rather than the pleasure of Jesus' will in and over their lives. Nevertheless, within our churches there are those who truly have this *hunger and thirst* for the Lord. They desire to walk before the Lord in *righteousness,* but when it comes to our own righteousness we have a problem.

Isaiah 64:6 But we are all like an unclean thing, and all our righteousnesses are like filthy rags; we all fade as a leaf, and our iniquities, like the wind, have taken us away.

This *righteousness* that we are to *hunger and thirst* for is not obtainable in our own flesh. There is nothing that we can do in and of ourselves to become righteous before the Lord, apart from His work in our lives. This is where Jesus comes in because Jesus accomplished for us what we could not do for ourselves, by saving us in His own righteousness.

Isaiah 59:17 For He put on righteousness as a breastplate, and a helmet of salvation on His head; He put on the garments of vengeance for clothing, and was clad with zeal as a cloak.

It is because of Jesus' work on the cross, where He bore our sins, that this righteousness, which can only come from God, has been made available to us.

Philippians 3:8b that I may gain Christ 9 and be found in Him, not having my own righteousness, which is from the law, but that which is through faith in Christ, the righteousness which is from God by faith.

We must each come to the realization that in our flesh, there dwells no good thing and that all our righteousness is like filthy rags before God. Even with all these things against us, we must still *hunger and thirst for righteousness.* Not our own righteousness, but the righteousness of Christ.

Blessed are we who obtain His righteousness, for we have this assurance from the Lord that we shall *be filled.*

Blessed Are the Merciful

Matthew 5:7 Blessed are the merciful, for they shall obtain mercy.

In this fifth declaration of blessedness, Jesus promises *mercy* to those who *are merciful.*

As believers we are not to be *merciful* to others in order that we may obtain *mercy* from others. We are to be *merciful* to others because we have already obtained *mercy* from God through the salvation that we have received by placing our faith in His Son, our Savior, Jesus Christ.

In the Bible we learn that God spoke to Moses *face to face, as a man speaks to his friend (Ex. 33:11),* but Moses desired more than just a conversation with God, he wanted to see His glory. However, before God allowed His goodness to pass before Moses, He first placed him in a cleft of a rock and covered him until He had passed by. Afterward, God removed His hand to allow Moses to see His back or His afterglow. It was while God passed by that He proclaimed His name. Contained within God's name are seven attributes, of which *mercy* is the first.

Ex 34:6-7 "The LORD, the LORD God, merciful and gracious, longsuffering, and abounding in goodness and truth, keeping mercy for thousands, forgiving iniquity and transgression and sin, by no means clearing the guilty, visiting the iniquity of the fathers upon the children and the children's children to the third and the fourth generation."

The psalmist David describes our LORD as being *abundant in mercy (Ps 86:5, 15).* Such is His *mercy* that it reaches into the heavens, rather above the heavens.

Ps 108:4 For Your mercy is great above the heavens, and Your truth reaches to the clouds.

David was able to extol the mercies of our LORD because he experienced God's *mercy* first hand when he cried, *"Have mercy upon me, O God, according to Your lovingkindness; according to the multitude of Your tender mercies, blot out my transgressions. Wash me thoroughly from my iniquity, and cleanse me from my sin" (Ps 51:1-2).* And God mercifully answered David's prayer.

Mercy is receiving from Jesus that which we do not deserve.

Eph 2:4 But God, who is rich in mercy, because of His great love with which He loved us...

God, in His rich mercy, sent his only begotten Son to die on a cross for our sins, so that we might abound in the mercies of God. Since we have already obtained the mercy of God through Jesus, we should likewise show mercy to others. Our mercies towards others need not be deserved because His mercies towards us have never been deserved. We show mercy because He has shown us mercy. We *who once were not a people but are now the people of God, who had not obtained mercy but now have obtained mercy (1 Pet 2:10).*

It is possible that we will error in showing mercy, but if we are going to err, let us err on the side of mercy. Better to show mercy and be wrong, than to judge and condemn someone who has truly repented of their wrong. Better to show mercy because we desire mercy and have received mercy from our merciful Savior, Jesus Christ our Lord.

Lam 3:22 Through the LORD's mercies we are not consumed, because His compassions fail not. 23b They are new every morning.

Blessed Are the Pure In Heart

Matthew 5:8 Blessed are the pure in heart, for they shall see God.

In this sixth declaration of blessedness, Jesus promises that the *pure in heart* will see God. However, herein lies our problem, because purity of heart is something we cannot obtain apart from Jesus Christ.

The Bible teaches that when God destroyed the world by the Flood *that the wickedness of man was great and that every intent of the thoughts of his heart was only evil continually (Gen 6:5).* Sadly, the condition of man's heart didn't improve any after the Flood. For in *Genesis 8:21* we read, *"And the LORD smelled a soothing aroma* (of Noah's offering).*" Then the LORD said in His heart, "I will never again curse the ground for man's sake, although the imagination of man's heart is evil from his youth; nor will I again destroy every living thing as I have done."*

I believe that we are living in the age that Jesus described in *Matthew 24:37-39,* saying, *"But as the days of Noah were, so also will the coming of the Son of Man be. For as in the days before the Flood, they were eating and drinking, marrying and giving in marriage, until the day that Noah entered into the ark, and did not know until the Flood came and took them all away, so also will the coming of the Son of Man be."*

As we recognize that the condition of our world is the same as in the days of Noah, we also must realize that our basic problem is the same as in the days of Noah. We have a heart condition, but so many of us are unaware of this condition.

The Psalmist David realized the condition of his heart and cried *"Create in me a clean heart, O God, and renew a steadfast spirit within me" (Ps 51:10).*

This clean or pure heart can only come by faith in Jesus Christ. John tells us that *it is the blood of Jesus Christ that cleanses us from all sin (1 Jn 1:7).* Therefore, as we each place our faith in Jesus, our hearts are made pure.

Acts 15:8 So God, who knows the heart, acknowledged them by giving them the Holy Spirit, just as He did to us, 9 and made no distinction between us and them, purifying their hearts by faith.

What a beautiful picture. God who knows that *every intent of the thoughts of our hearts are only evil continually* and *that the imagination of man's heart is evil from his youth,* is willing to purify our hearts through faith in His Son, Jesus!

God acknowledging us as pure is called, "Positional Sanctification." It is a position that we have in Jesus, but God also desires us to be pure in this present world, which is called, "Practical Sanctification."

David asked, *"How can a young man cleanse his way? By taking heed according to Your word" (Ps 119:9).*

Jesus said, *"You are already clean because of the word which I have spoken to you" (Jn 15:3).*

Paul wrote, *"that He might sanctify and cleanse her with the washing of water by the word" (Eph 5:26).*

Blessed are the pure in heart, blessed meaning a *spiritual well-being and prosperity, a deep joy of the soul.* Why do the *pure in heart* have this blessing? Because one day they *shall see God!*

Blessed Are the Peacemakers

Matthew 5:9 Blessed are the peacemakers, for they shall be called sons of God.

In this seventh declaration of blessedness, Jesus promises that *the peacemakers shall be called sons of God.*

Peacemakers are those who help bring harmonious relationships between mankind. There are many who attempt to bring peace apart from God. The Peace Corp comes to mind as well as many other private or government funded agencies. Their work is good and noble, but the peace they bring is a false peace, built upon the fallacy that mankind will continue to improve their environment and the condition of their surroundings until they reach utopia. The prophet Jeremiah gives us a great example of this style of peacemaking.

Jer 6:14 They have also healed the hurt of My people slightly, saying, 'Peace, peace!' when there is no peace.

Jer 6:14 And they have healed the brokenness of My people superficially, saying, 'Peace, peace,' but there is no peace. NASB

Jer 6:14 They dress the wound of my people as though it were not serious. 'Peace, peace,' they say, when there is no peace. NIV

Although many things have improved in our lives, there are many more things that are beyond our control. It seems when we succeed in one area, there are always a countless number of other areas that threaten to destroy our lives.

The 12/31/99 issue of USA Today called AIDS, influenza, polio and small pox, *"the four horsemen of the apocalypse... four killers that stalked the twentieth century."*

Now that we are several years into the 21st century, we find that as some of these *pestilences* seem to be coming under control, there are a countless number of new pandemics threatening to take our lives. Not to mention the *wars and rumors of wars, famines and earthquakes* that daily seem to be in our news stories.

What are we to do? Our only hope is in the *Prince of Peace* who gave His life to bring us into a harmonious relationship with God.

Eph 2:14 For He Himself is our peace, who has made both one, and has broken down the middle wall of separation, 15 having abolished in His flesh the enmity, that is, the law of commandments contained in ordinances, so as to create in Himself one new man from the two, thus making peace, 16 and that He might reconcile them both to God in one body through the cross, thereby putting to death the enmity. 17 And He came and preached peace to you who were afar off and to those who were near. 18 For through Him we both have access by one Spirit to the Father.

It is not that we shouldn't be about the business of easing the physical suffering that we see in this world. However, as we ease the physical plight of our brothers and sisters, we should be concerned about their spiritual condition as well. We are true *peacemakers* when we help bring others into a right relationship with Jesus Christ - the Prince of Peace.

Paul tells us in *Romans 5:1, "We have peace with God through our Lord Jesus Christ."* So it is necessary to *"Go into all the world and preach the gospel to every creature" (Mk 16:15)* and present to them *the Prince of Peace (Is. 6:9).* For those who do so will be called the sons of God!

Blessed Are the Persecuted

Matthew 5:10 Blessed are those who are persecuted for righteousness' sake, for theirs is the kingdom of heaven. 11 Blessed are you when they revile and persecute you, and say all kinds of evil against you falsely for My sake. 12 Rejoice and be exceedingly glad, for great is your reward in heaven, for so they persecuted the prophets who were before you.

In this eighth and final declaration of blessedness, Jesus promises the kingdom of heaven to those who are persecuted.

Although persecution is nothing that any of us desires, when it does come, we have the assurance of Jesus that our reward in heaven will be great. Persecution also places us in some very good company, *for so they persecuted the prophets who were before* us.

The righteous are reviled, persecuted and spoken evil of, as a result of their relationship with Jesus. *Dikaios* (dik`-ah-yos) is the root of the Greek word from which we translate the word *righteousness*. It speaks about having *integrity, virtue* or a *purity of life* that reaches into every area of a person's being; affecting their thoughts, emotions and actions.

Jesus used this word five times during the Sermon on the Mount.

5:6 Refers to those who *hunger and thirst for <u>righteousness.</u>*

5:10 Refers to those *who are persecuted for <u>righteousness'</u> sake.*

5:20 Jesus told His disciples that if their righteousness did not *exceed the <u>righteousness</u> of the scribes and Pharisees* that they would not *enter into the kingdom of God.*

22

6:33 Jesus warns that if our *charitable deeds* are done to be seen by others, we will have no heavenly reward.

6:33 Seeking first the kingdom of God and His righteousness is the climax of understanding the type of righteousness that God desires from us.

It is not our *righteousness* that we must *hunger and thirst for.* It is not our *righteousness* that should result in our being persecuted. It is not our *righteousness* that should *exceed the righteousness of the scribes and Pharisees.* It is not our *righteousness* that should be magnified when we do a *charitable deed.*

Isa 64:6 But we are all like an unclean thing, and all our righteousness are like filthy rags; we all fade as a leaf, and our iniquities, like the wind, have taken us away.

It is *His righteousness* that we must *hunger and thirst for.* It is because of *His righteousness* that persecution will come. It is only *His righteousness* that will *exceed the righteousness of* all others. It is because of *Jesus' righteousness* working through us that we do *charitable deeds* in secret which brings glory to the Father, who will *reward us openly.*

Phil 3:8b That I may gain Christ 9 and be found in Him, not having my own righteousness, which is from the law, but that which is through faith in Christ, the righteousness which is from God by faith.

For those of us who have put on *the righteousness of God, through faith in Jesus Christ,* rejoice and be glad, for He has promised that ours *is the kingdom of heaven.*

Matt 7:21 Not everyone who says to Me, 'Lord, Lord,' shall enter the kingdom of heaven, but he who does the will of My Father in heaven.

The Four Beatitudes of Luke

Luke 6:20 Then He lifted up His eyes toward His disciples, and said: "Blessed are you poor, for yours is the kingdom of God. 21 Blessed are you who hunger now, for you shall be filled. Blessed are you who weep now, for you shall laugh. 22 Blessed are you when men hate you, and when they exclude you, and revile you, and cast out your name as evil, for the Son of Man's sake. 23 Rejoice in that day and leap for joy! For indeed your reward is great in heaven, for in like manner their fathers did to the prophets."

Luke gives us an abbreviated teaching in comparison to Matthew, but in both teachings we find that the circumstances of life are only temporary for those who believe.

As in Matthew's gospel, Jesus promises that the poor will be given the kingdom of heaven, those who hunger will be filled, those who weep will laugh and those who are hated, excluded, reviled and whose names are cast out for Jesus' sake will be given great heavenly reward. Furthermore, instead of being angry about the persecutions that might come our way, Jesus told us to *rejoice in that day and leap for joy! For indeed your reward is great in heaven, for in like manner their fathers did to the prophets.*

Jesus places the hated, excluded, reviled and those whose names are cast out in the company of the prophets of old! However, we are not to rejoice and leap for joy because we are persecuted, but because our reward is great in heaven!

2 Cor 12:10 Therefore I take pleasure in infirmities, in reproaches, in needs, in persecutions, in distresses, for Christ's sake. For when I am weak, then I am strong.

The Four Woes of Luke

Although Luke's teaching on the Beatitudes may be abbreviated in comparison to Matthew, he adds to the teaching by giving us four woes concerning those who do not believe.

1. The First Woe

Luke 6:24 But woe to you who are rich, for you have received your consolation.

It is not a sin to be rich, but it is a sin to place our trust in riches. In *Luke 12:13-21*, Jesus told a parable of a certain rich man who was blessed with a bumper crop. However, his great blessing did not spur him to share with the less fortunate. Instead, he planned to pull down his old barns to build larger ones, saying, *"Soul, you have many goods laid up for many years; take your ease; eat, drink, and be merry."* Little did he know on that very night he would die, which caused God to ask, *"Then whose will those things be which you have provided?"* To this Jesus remarked, *"So is he who lays up treasure for himself, and is not rich toward God."*

On the other hand, Paul instructed Timothy concerning those who are rich, of how they might be rich toward God, *saying, "Command those who are rich in this present age not to be haughty, nor to trust in uncertain riches but in the living God, who gives us richly all things to enjoy. Let them do good, that they be rich in good works, ready to give, willing to share, storing up for themselves a good foundation for the time to come, that they may lay hold on eternal life" (1 Tim 6:17-19).*

Those who are rich in this life with no concern for others and the things of God will discover that their reward will be limited to this side of heaven, for they have already received their consolation and thus rejected the kingdom of God.

2. The Second Woe

Luke 6:25a Woe to you who are full, for you shall hunger.

In *Luke 16:19-31,* Jesus told of a certain rich man and a beggar named Lazarus. The rich man *was clothed in purple and fine linen and fared sumptuously every day.* In contrast, *Lazarus* was *full of sores,* and has *laid at* the rich man's *gate, desiring to be fed with the crumbs which fell from* his *table.* To make matters worse, the dogs came and licked his sores.

After they died, they found their roles reversed, for Lazarus *was carried by the angels to Abraham's bosom,* while the rich man was buried and found himself in the torments of Hades.

Now the rich man became the beggar, saying to Abraham, *"Send Lazarus that he may dip the tip of his finger in water and cool my tongue; for I am tormented in this flame." "But Abraham said, 'Son, remember that in your lifetime you received your good things, and likewise Lazarus evil things; but now he is comforted and you are tormented.'"*

He also begged that Abraham would send someone back to warn his brothers of the torments of hell. To which Abraham said, *"They have Moses and the prophets; let them hear them."*

Finally, he begged that Abraham would send one who had risen from the dead, reasoning that his brothers would believe one who had risen again. To this Abraham responded, *"If they do not hear Moses and the prophets, neither will they be persuaded though one rise from the dead."*

Those who are full in this life will find that they will hunger after they die. In contrast, those who hunger in faith toward Jesus will one day be filled. For He promised us, saying, *"I am the bread of life. He who comes to Me shall never hunger, and he who believes in Me shall never thirst" (Jn 6:35).*

26

3. The Third Woe

Luke 6:25b Woe to you who laugh now, for you shall mourn and weep.

Laughter before God signifies pride, while weeping acknowledges God's rule over our lives. Their laugher will be turned into mourning and weeping, because after they die, they will discover that they had forsaken God's gift of grace which He had made available to them through His Son, Jesus Christ.

Better to do as James instructs us: *"Lament and mourn and weep! Let your laughter be turned to mourning and your joy to gloom. Humble yourselves in the sight of the Lord, and He will lift you up" (Jam 4:9-10).* Only through Jesus will we find that our weeping will be turned into laughter.

4. The Fourth Woe

Luke 6:26 Woe to you when all men speak well of you, for so did their fathers to the false prophets.

It is a very dangerous thing to receive the praises of others, for in doing so, we can be lifted up with pride. As Solomon taught us, *"Pride goes before destruction, and a haughty spirit before a fall" (Prov 16:18).*

The forefathers of these men had spoken well of the false prophets, which is a warning to us that just because others may speak well of someone, it does not mean that their ways are right.

Better to be hated, excluded, reviled and to have our names cast out, than to be well spoken of on earth and lose our great heavenly reward. For such hatred form others places us in the company of Jesus, who said, *"If the world hates you, you know that it hated Me before it hated you" (Jn 15:18).*

Closing

As we have looked at The Beatitudes, it seems odd that Jesus should use such a word as blessed to describe a person who may be the poor in spirit, the mournful, the meek, the hungry and thirsty or the persecuted. It seems odd, but only at first glance because Jesus concludes each of these situations with a promise of an absolute surety that our condition is only temporary!

Therefore, the poor in spirit will obtain the kingdom of heaven. The mournful will find comfort. The meek will inherit the earth. Those who are hungry and thirsty for righteousness will be filled. The merciful shall obtain mercy. The pure in heart shall see God. The peacemakers shall be called the sons of God and those who are persecuted for righteousness' sake, theirs is the kingdom of heaven.

All the above promises are for those who have realized their need for Jesus and the salvation that He provides to everyone who seeks His face. It is my prayer that you have accepted Jesus as your personal Lord and Savior. If you have, then all the promises of The Beatitudes are available to you. However, if you have never asked Jesus to be the Lord and Savior over your life, then will you consider doing so today?

All you need to do is:

1. Recognize that you are a sinner. *Rom 3:23, Rom 6:23*
2. Realize that Jesus died for you. *Rom 5:8*
3. Repent of your sins. *Rom 10:9-10*
4. Receive Jesus as your Lord and Savior. *Rev 3:20*
5. Acknowledge Jesus before others. *Luke 12:8-9*
6. Don't wait another day! *2 Cor 6:2*

The Beatitudes

Matthew 5:1-12

1 And seeing the multitudes, He went up on a mountain, and when He was seated His disciples came to Him.

2 Then He opened His mouth and taught them, saying:

3 Blessed are the poor in spirit, for theirs is the kingdom of heaven.

4 Blessed are those who mourn, for they shall be comforted.

5 Blessed are the meek, for they shall inherit the earth.

6 Blessed are those who hunger and thirst for righteousness, for shall be filled.

7 Blessed are the merciful, for they shall obtain mercy.

8 Blessed are the pure in heart, for they shall see God.

9 Blessed are the peacemakers, for they shall be called sons of God.

10 Blessed are those who are persecuted for righteousness' sake, for theirs is the kingdom of heaven.

11 Blessed are you when they revile and persecute you, and say all kinds of evil against you falsely for My sake.

12 Rejoice and be exceedingly glad, for great is your reward in heaven, for so they persecuted the prophets who were before you.

What We Believe

Calvary Chapel has been formed as a fellowship of believers in the Lordship of Jesus Christ. Our greatest desire is to know Christ and to be conformed into His image by the power of the Holy Spirit.

We are not a denominational church, nor are we opposed to denominations as such, only their over-emphasis of the doctrinal differences that divide of the Body of Christ.

We believe that the only true basis of Christian fellowship is His (Agape) love, which is greater than any differences we possess and without which we have no right to claim ourselves Christians.

We believe worship of God should be spiritual. Therefore, we remain flexible and yielded to the leading of the Holy Spirit to direct our worship.

We believe worship of God should be inspirational. Therefore, we give a great place to music in our worship.

We believe worship of God should be intelligent. Therefore, our services are designed with great emphasis upon teaching the Word of God that He might instruct us how He should be worshiped.

We believe worship of God is fruitful. Therefore, we look for His love in our lives as the supreme manifestation that we have truly been worshiping Him.

Notes

Notes